Jake's C

Story by Annette Smith
Photography by Lindsay Edwards

Rigby®

A Harcourt Achieve Imprint

www.Rigby.com
1-800-531-5015

Jake said to Dad,

"Come and look

at my car."

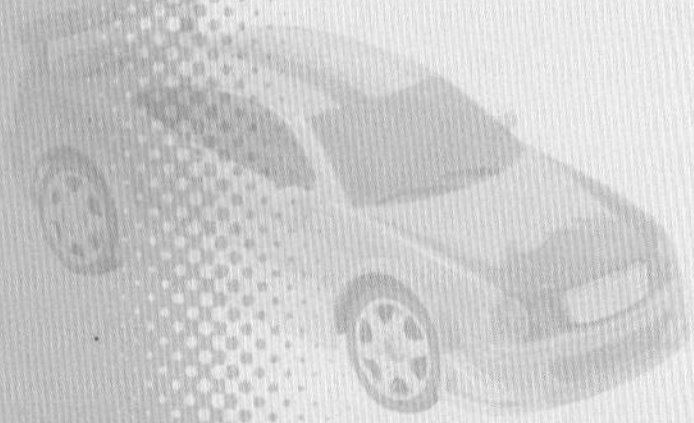

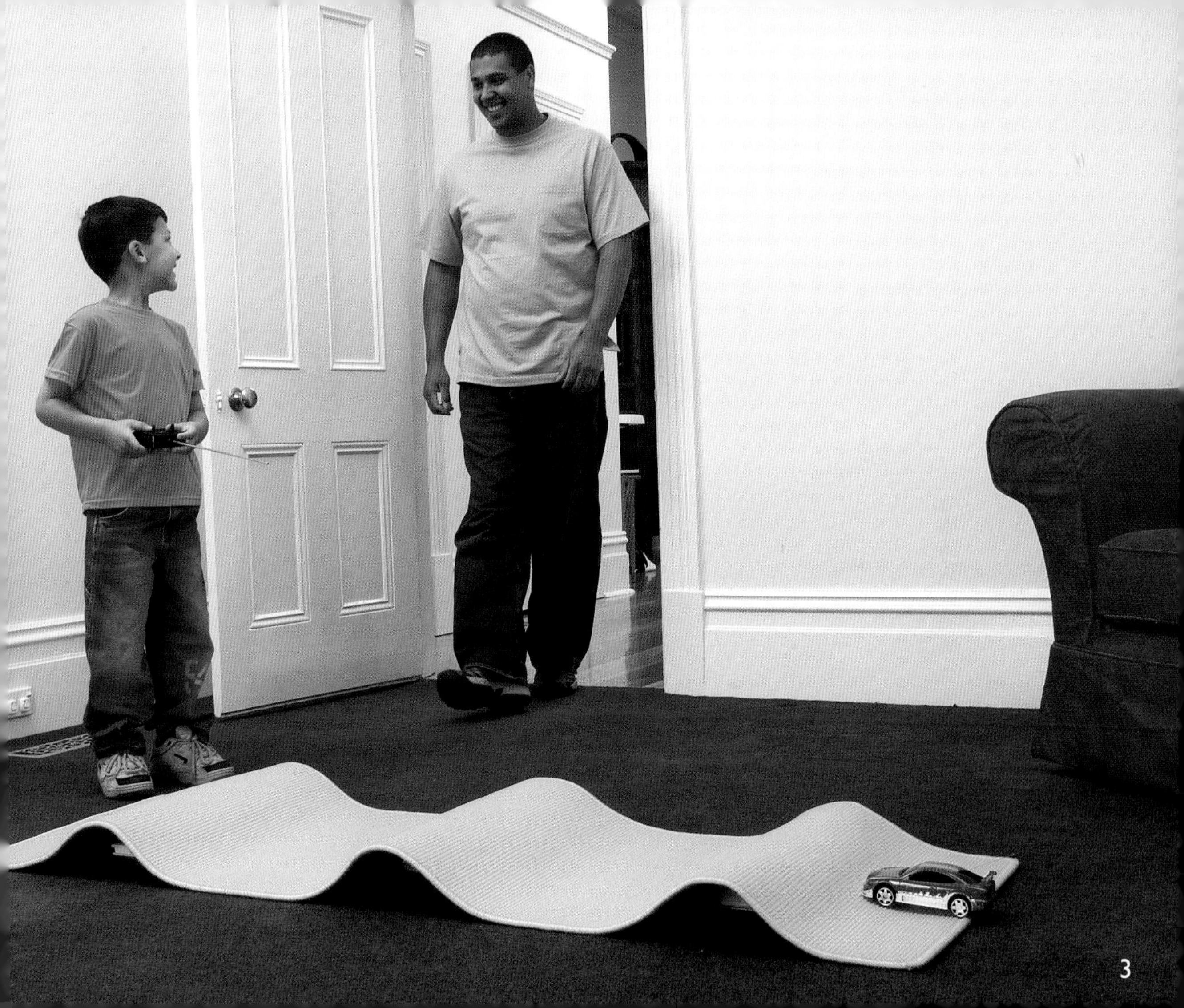

"My car can go

up and down the hills,"

said Jake.

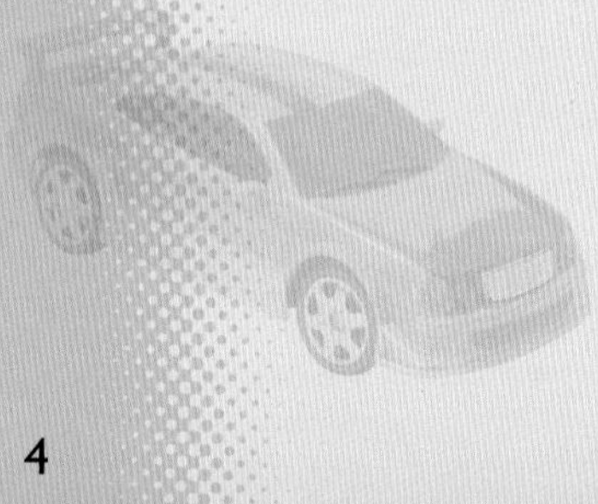

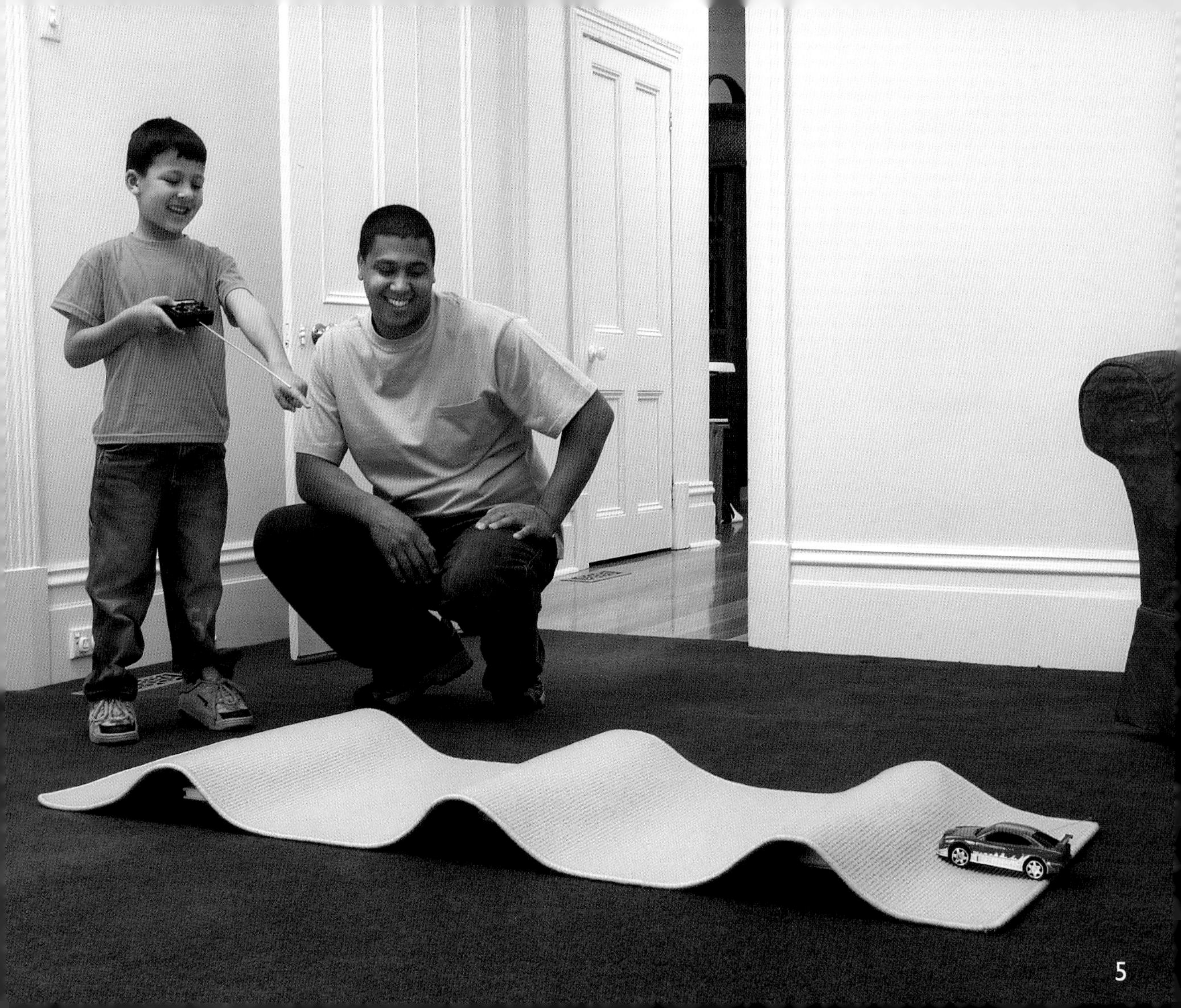

"Look, Dad!" said Jake.

"My car is going

up and down and up . . .

Oh no!

My car is **not** going!"

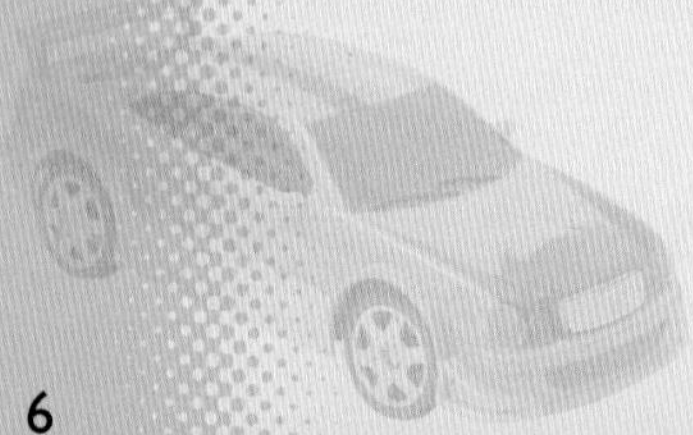

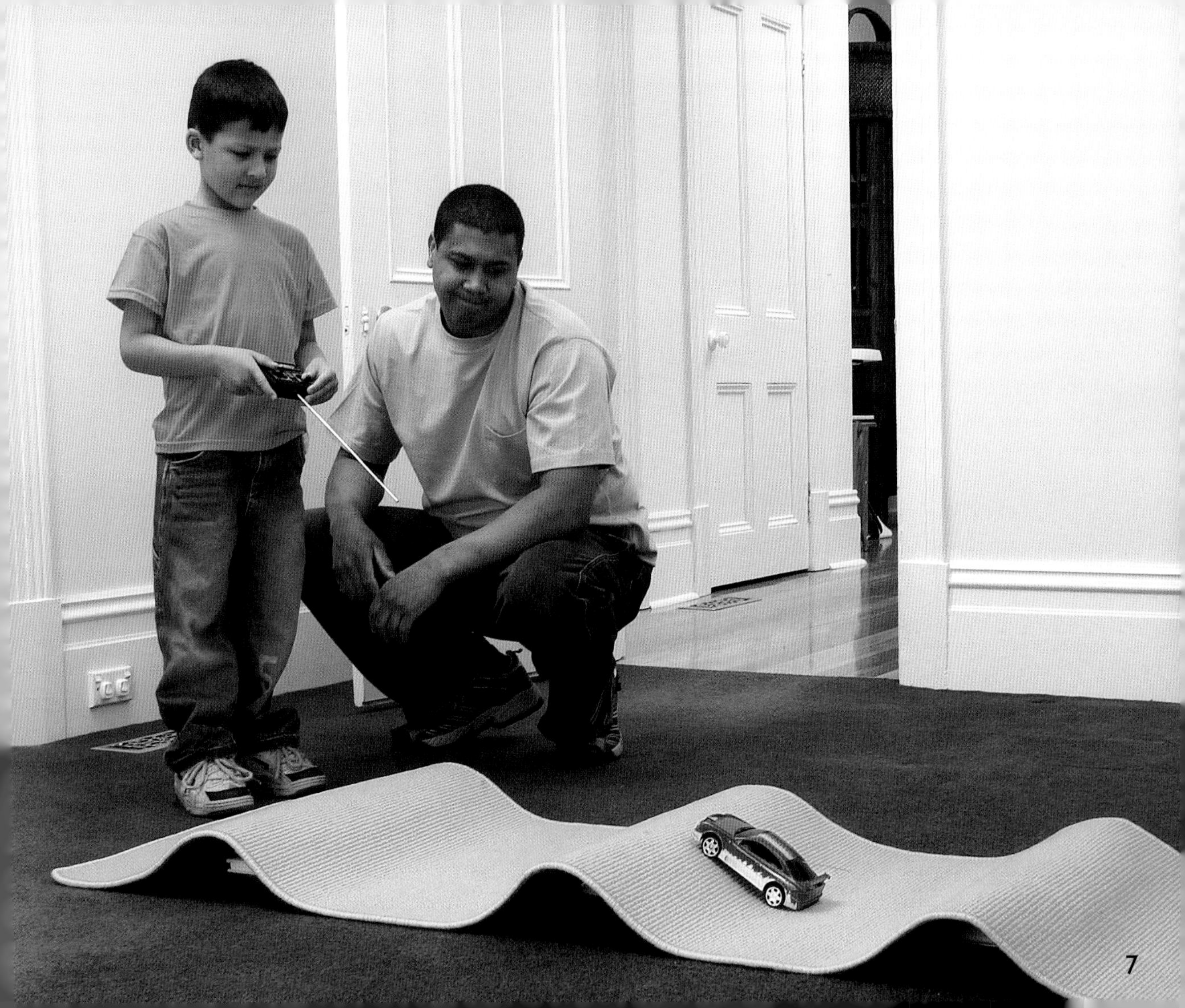

Jake looked at the car.

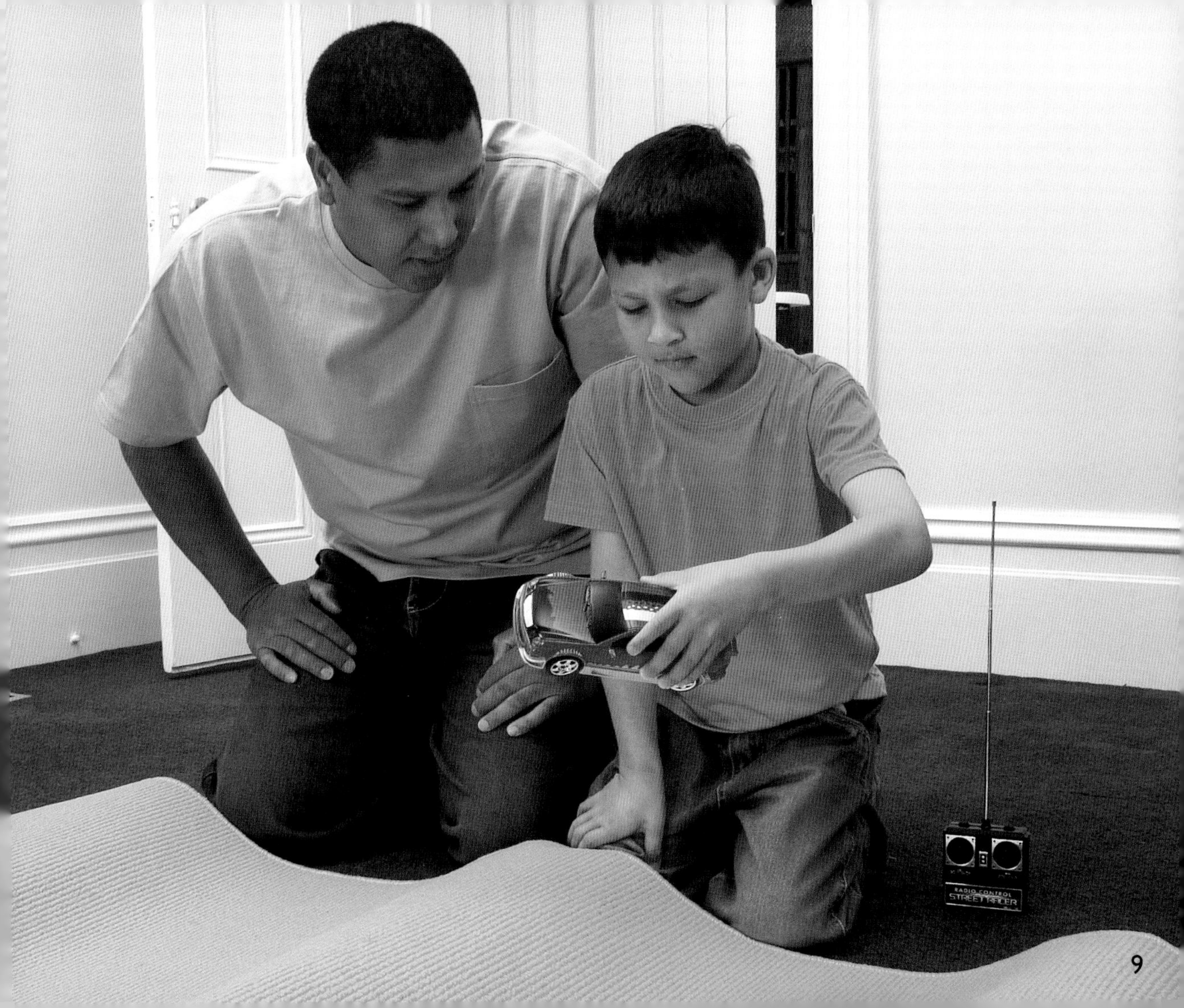
RADIO CONTROL
STREET RACER

Dad looked **in** the car.

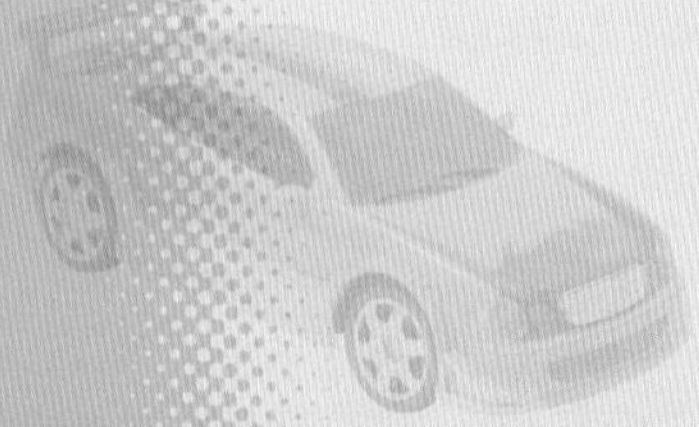

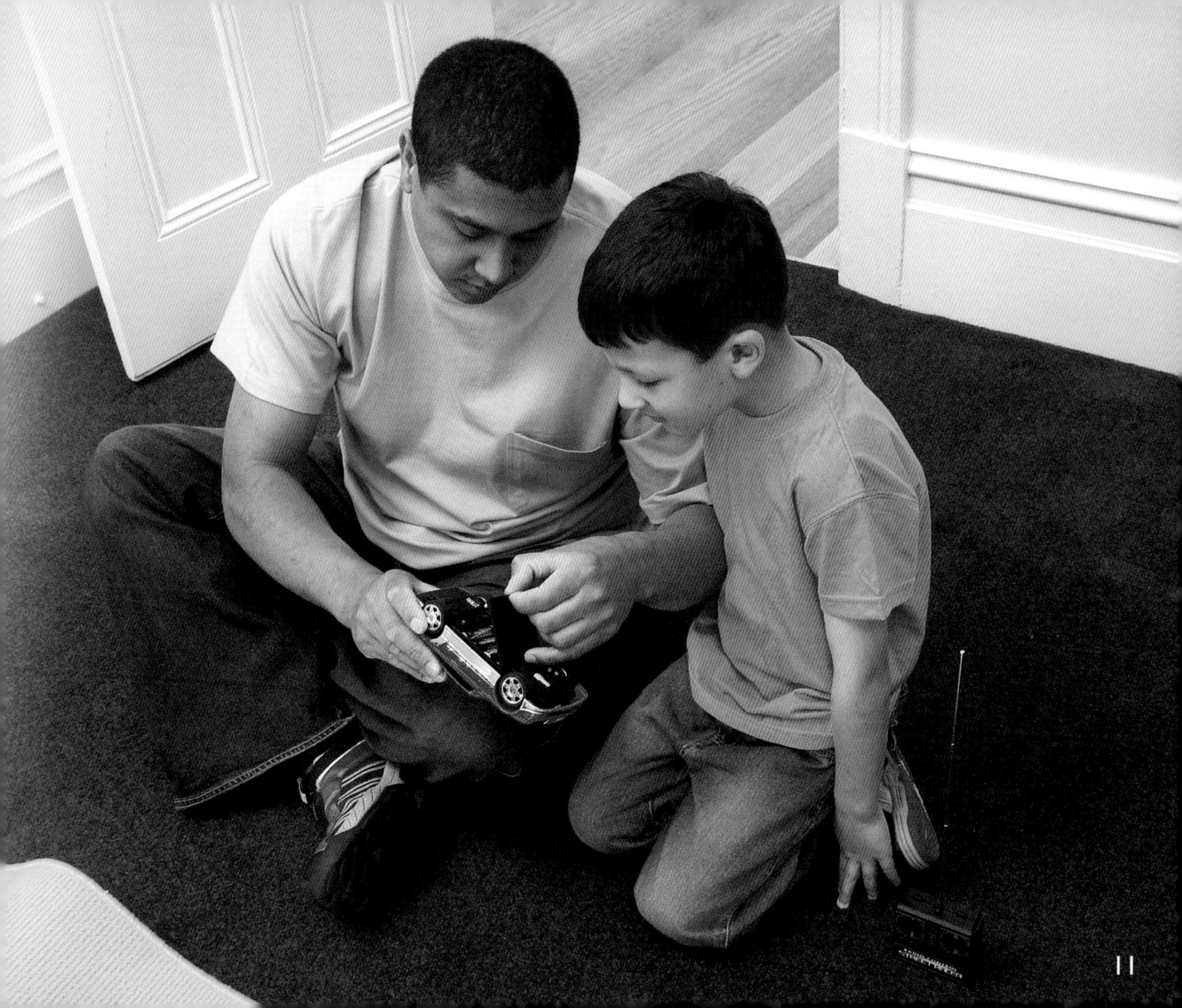

Dad said,

"Here are four little batteries

for the car, Jake."

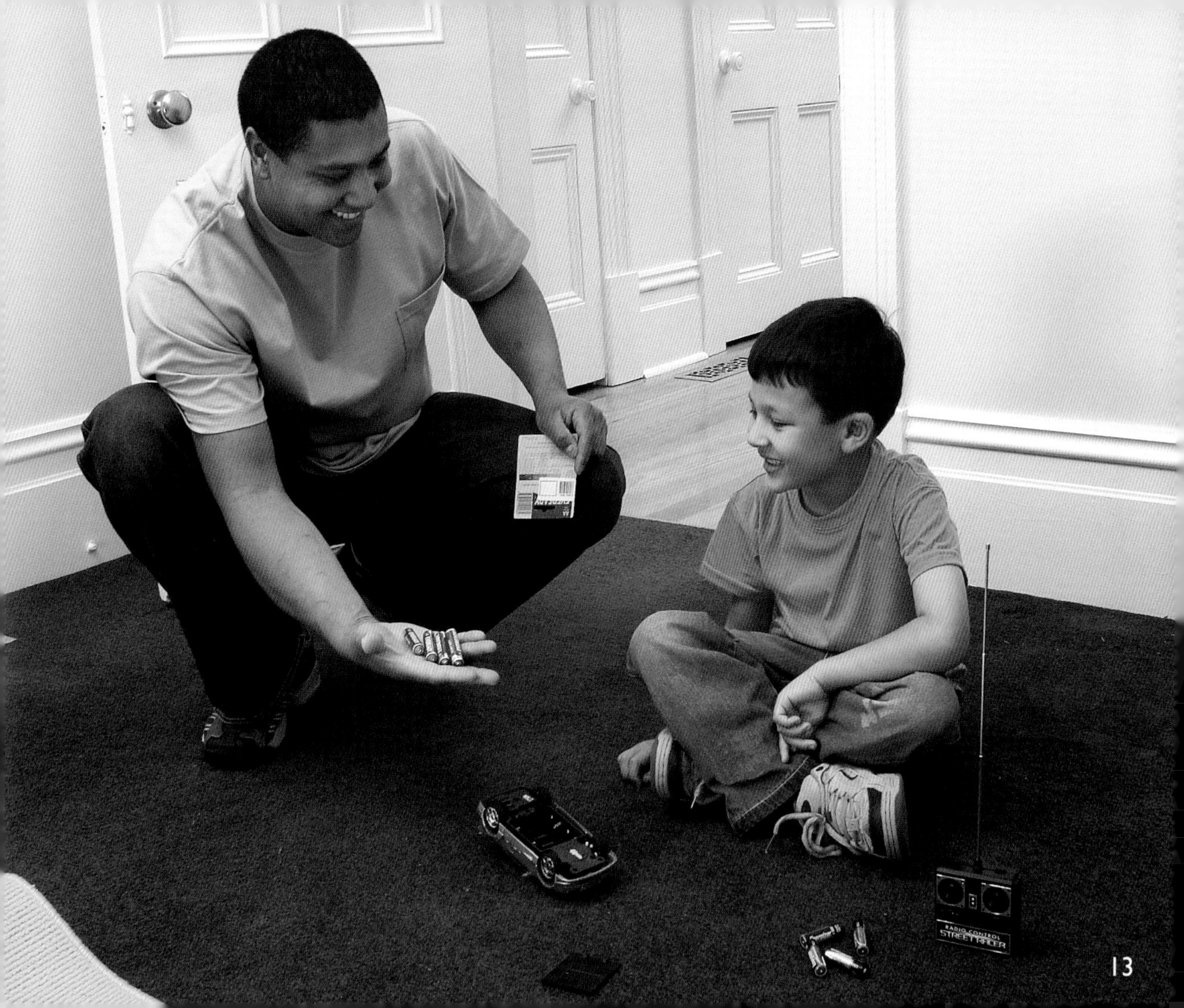
RADIO CONTROL
STREETRACER

“Look at my car, Dad!”

said Jake.

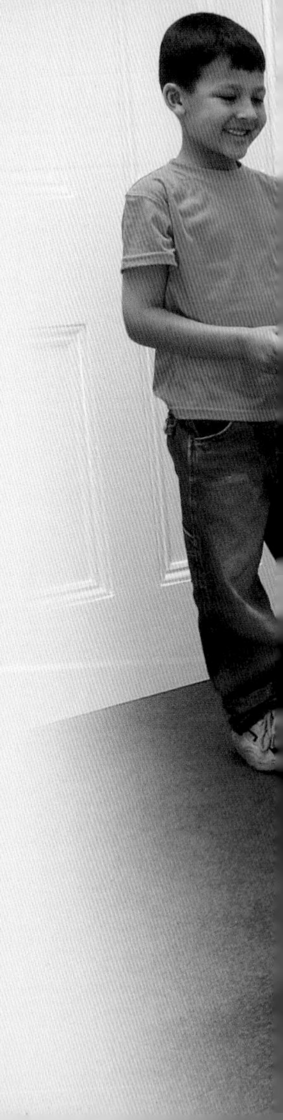

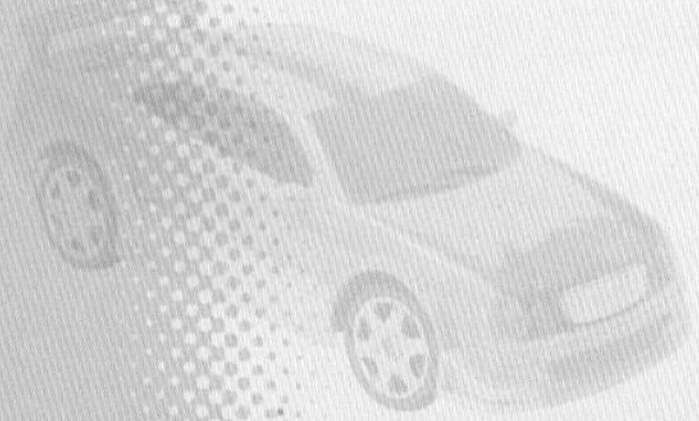

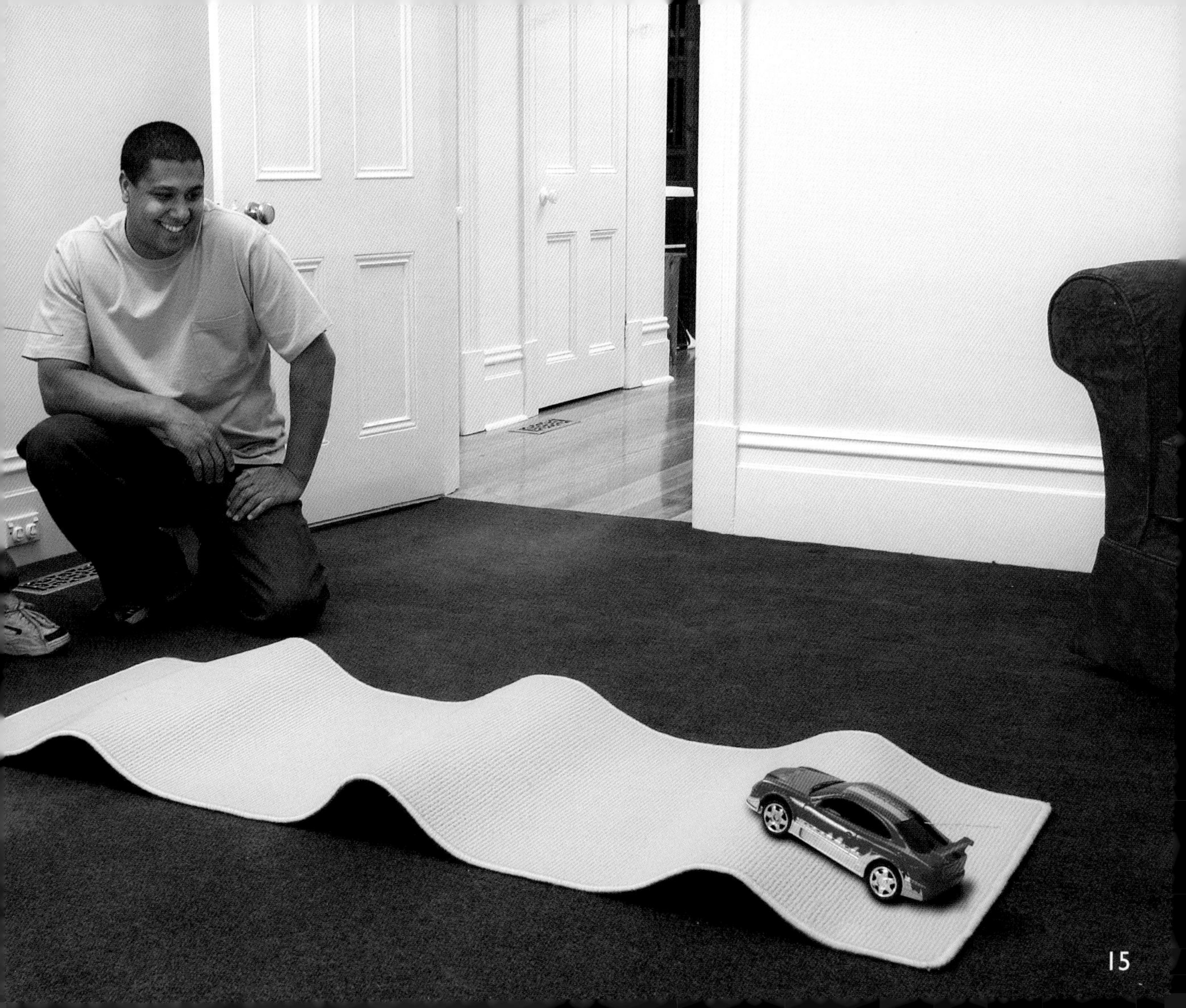

"My car is going up and down the hills!" said Jake.

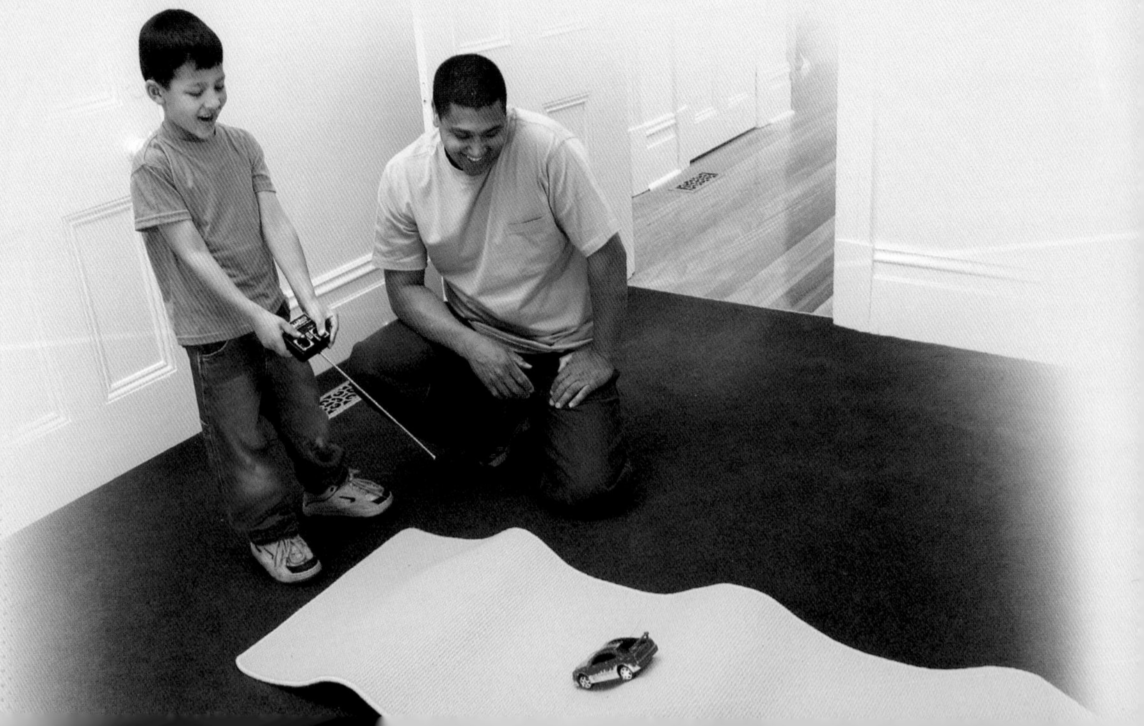